WISDOM
WORTH
SPREADING

Everyday Wisdom to Navigate the
Journey of Life

MOHAMMED HAKIM

***

"They say, "there is a whole world out there", but truly, there is a whole world "in here", inside of you, as you will realize that the greatest source of power and truth comes from within you if you take the time to get to know yourself. Dive deep into the book and find yourself."

Ioana Gheorghiu,
Author of between soul & bone

***

"This book is raw and revolutionary. It is a clarion cry, an 11th hour wake up call, to honestly evaluate why we do what we do. This is a must read for anyone who wants to come to terms with ULTIMATE reality, embrace ultimate truth and learn how to shape and order their lives around it. AMAZING!"

Angee Costa,
Author of Otherlen: Tale of a Dreamfaller

***

"Mindful and heartfelt, this book is an ode to a father's love for his son. Chock-full of nuggets of wisdom that we all would do better to keep in mind on this journey called life."

A Friend,
Anonymous

Table of Contents

Preface... 1

Introduction 3

PART-1 Wisdom..5

    Chapter 1: Life 7

    Chapter 2: Friends and Enemies...............................17

    Chapter 3: Life's Purpose...25

    Chapter 4: Time and Money.....................................31

    Chapter 5: Understanding Yourself and Others.........39

PART-II Application of the Wisdom 51

    Chapter 6: Success, Power, and Happiness 59

    Chapter 7: Creating Your Own Life 67

    Chapter 8: Artificial World......................................79

    Chapter 9: How to Bring the Change........................91

    Chapter 10: How to Win the Game of Life 97

Conclusion 101

Acknowledgements 103

About the Author..105

PREFACE

The Blueprint for Building This Book

There better be a good reason for one more book on life to be written, right?

The way I originally conceptualized this book was as a series of letters from a father (me) to his newborn son (mine), in which the father explains what life is all about. These letters have been adapted into chapters so that they might be shared with the world in the form of a book. It's said that wisdom and knowledge always increase when it is shared with others. It's my heartfelt hope and wish that this book can help others find meaning in their life. If I can inspire, change, motivate even a single person on this earth through this book, I would consider my life worth living.

When a man's wife gets pregnant, it tends to set off some pretty deep thoughts in his brain. As I pondered over my changing life, I had a saddening realization: that, because my time on this Earth may end at any time, I have no idea how much I have to spend with my child and to see him grow. I may not have enough time to share with him all the wisdom which I wish to. That's a risk I don't want to take.

Thus I began writing letters to my soon-to-be-born son. At the time of putting together this book, my wife was due in a few short weeks; the sense of urgency spurred me to complete the project in ten days. I kept all my letters very short and straight to the point. I intentionally did so in order to make sure I would share only the most important lessons and in as few words as possible.

This book is for anyone who wishes to unveil the difficult answers to life's difficult questions and who feels the need to learn practical wisdom to apply in their daily life. To preserve the original essence of the letters, each chapter is addressed directly to my son, but the advice contained herein is applicable to everyone experiencing this journey called life.

INTRODUCTION

Dear son,

As I write this page, you are sleeping comfortably inside your mother's belly. Soon you will enter this wonderful but at times crazy world. Ever since we found out about your existence, I have been thinking about what I, as your father, can provide you that will stay with you for your whole life, long after I am gone. I decided on this book. It is a brief book attempted by a common man to spread his simple, commonsense, everyday wisdom. There lies certain wisdom in every aspect of experiencing life, and everyone living on this earth has encountered it. Whether they look it in the face is a different matter.

This book is full of my honest views on factors of human existence, such as people, relationships, business, life's purpose, emotions, fear, love, greed, and more. It is divided into ten chapters, but to understand the message, you have to collectively understand the whole as one; they are not ten separate messages but rather one message explained from ten perspectives. My hope is that by gaining this knowledge, you will find it easier to navigate your journey.

My earnest intention is to discuss the truth and only the truth, nothing else. It is to offer you a blueprint from which you may know yourself better and, consequently, know the world better. In these pages, there exists a clear filter through which to see the world, truly see the world, and yourself in it, belonging to it and within it in a way that serves your highest joy and purpose. I do not expect that you would understand all of the concepts in a single reading. As you reread these concepts throughout different stages of your life, the wisdom will continue to unfold for you. I strongly recommend and desire that you read it every year on your birthday, refreshing your mind on the lessons learned here and cross-checking them with the actual reality of your life. Another important tip: do not pick up this book as a bedtime read. I repeat, please do not read it as a source of intellectual entertainment. If you seriously want to understand its contents in the spirit they are written, read this book early in the morning while the entire world around you is sleeping (which is exactly the way I wrote it). Read it in the sweet solitude of your own company, calm and undisturbed by the voices and chaos of the external world. I am confident that by doing so, you will grasp what I want to communicate to you.

Boy, welcome to the world! And now, let's begin this journey!

Much love,

Your father

PART-1

WISDOM

CHAPTER 1

LIFE

Now that you are here on this earth, traveling on the road called life, it's very important you understand what exactly life is all about. So the truth is, life is the journey straight towards death. It is a slow, beautiful, yet challenging journey towards death. Sorry for being so dramatic in the opening paragraph of the first letter. But son, that's the ultimate truth.

The sooner you realize this concept, the easier it will be for you to get comfortable with this world. This one simple concept will save you from a lot of misery. Living your life with humbleness, knowing that one day you will be departing this world, will keep you grounded. **You arrived naked and empty-handed in this world, and so will you leave.** Now that you are aware of this fact, consider yourself lucky. You will observe that most of humanity operates as though they were here on this earth for eternity. This simple realization will offer you a realistic perspective of the world and a keen eye for the things that truly matter. This realization will help you distinguish the madness of this world from the actual reality.

So what is the actual reality?

To understand the reality, let's first understand how your mind operates. Your mind constantly keeps you busy with thoughts, some wanted and others unwanted. Your mind creates an illusionary world—what I call an artificial, or delusionary, reality—by keeping you busy thinking about things that never occurred and might never occur. While your mind keeps you busy with thoughts, you are missing the moments that you are living and breathing. The moment to moment, each and every breath you take, is actual reality. This very moment when you are reading this sentence is actual reality. Everything else is an illusion. Be mindful of the present moment; it is the best and only gift. It only matters what you do now.

You will see that people compare someone's life to their age, as if the two are equivalent. They say, "Wow, this guy lived ninety years." But life is not about how many years you are here on this earth. It's about how many moments you are actually alive during those years, how present, and how aware were you of those moments -- no matter how short.

People often spend their entire lives dwelling in their pasts and worrying about their futures. While they are doing this, they forget to truly live in the moment. To understand life, you must understand the present. To enjoy life, enjoy this moment. Live life from now, moment to moment, welcoming each experience of life as it unfolds its **nature** to you moment to moment.

The Nature of Life

If I were to teach you only one word from the English dictionary, it would be *impermanence*.

Noun: *impermanence*
- *"the state or quality of enduring for a limited period of time."*

Adjective: *impermanent*
- *"not permanent or enduring; transitory."*

Son, remember **the nature of life is impermanence**, and this is the ultimate truth.

Let's take a look at this concept from a different angle. If you observe carefully, you will notice that nothing around you is still. Everything is in a constant state of change, either by form or by motion. Day fades to night; night fades back to the day. The planet's seasons switch from summer to fall to winter to spring, and the cycle repeats. The entire geography of the earth has been in a constant state of transformation for billions of years. Looking at the bigger picture, outer space is in contact movement as well: planets revolve around stars, stars burn, and countless other phenomena occur every single moment everywhere in the universe.

Now let's look at ourselves. Starting with conception, our physical body is constantly changing—from infant, to toddler, to teen, to adulthood, to old age. This is very apparent when we look at photos taken twenty years apart, for example, but the reality is that we are changing every fraction of every second. Trillions of cells which make up our body are dying and being replaced by new cells. We cannot perceive these small changes, of course.

Whatever you encounter in your life will have the same nature of impermanence. Your thoughts, your emotions, your feelings, your loved ones, and your surroundings, nothing will remain the same or still. **It is all in a constant state of transformation.**

You might ask, *How does this knowledge help me?*

Well, it helps you keep your emotional equilibrium. When you have a new experience, be it good or bad, positive or negative, you should never get too excited or too depressed. Always remember that whatever situation or environment you currently find yourself in, can and will change. This is the nature of life.

For example, if you encounter something to your liking — something attractive, beautiful, addictive, or anything which generates craving for your five senses — **aim not to get attached to the pleasant sensations it generates.** Experience it and enjoy it fully, but detach yourself from needing it to feel happy. This type of need or craving will make you feel as if you are always missing something in life. Enjoy things you like, but remember that you are ultimately the only source of your own happiness. Be a wise witness to your feelings and desires instead of a slave to them.

On the other side of the spectrum, for example, when you encounter anything you dislike — be it misery, suffering, any unpleasant situation or circumstance — **don't cultivate the feeling of aversion towards it.** Try to be non-judgmental and disidentify yourself from the negative feelings and emotions surrounding the situation. No matter how intense the situation is, it too, shall pass.

Always remember, nothing in this world is permanent. The best way to experience life is to have a very balanced and equanimous mind which neither craves pleasant sensations nor abhors negative sensations of the mind or body. The greater your equanimity and imperturbability, the more you are able to observe life as it is, the greater the clarity with which you will begin to look at life directly in its face.

The chapter entitled "Understanding Yourself and Others" will go into more detail about how keeping in mind the nature of life will help you understand yourself and the world better.

The Law of Nature

It's time you understand the law of all laws, also called the "law of nature" or the "law of the universe." Here it is:

"Nothing happens in the universe against the will of nature" – *and this is the ultimate truth.*

From the smallest particle of dust to the largest mass in outer space, everything works in accordance with the will of nature. Nothing can escape this law. Anything that you encounter in your life—from different; situations, to feelings, to surroundings, to people, to experiences—happens only if nature wishes so. Whatever nature intends has nothing to do with you or your wishes. You are powerless before nature's will. However, if you can work with it, it will be your greatest ally.

The logical question you might have at this juncture is, *Don't I have free will?*

Sure, you do, but your free will is limited to the boundaries of your body and mind. Once you are faced with a situation outside your body in the physical world, your individual free will is superseded by the will of nature.

Here is a clear example to better illustrate this concept:

You are planning to attend a friend's destination wedding. You are his best man, so you better be there. You have planned everything, from transportation to hotel accommodations to your speech. But on the day of your departure, it so happens through an unfortunate turn of events that you miss your flight. Maybe you forgot your passport, or you hit extraordinarily heavy traffic on the way to the airport, or your car won't start, or you fell ill, or a snowstorm sprang up. There's an endless number of permutations and combinations of possible events that are out of your control and due to which you might miss your flight.

Any one of these events, however, is not random; it is precisely calculated and well planned out by the will of nature. Our small and limited minds cannot fully understand the reasons behind these events, we must only trust with our hearts that what happened was for the best for everyone involved. Sometimes nature provides us with detours (that we sometimes perceive as inconveniences) that actually saves our life, protects us from danger, or guides us towards a circumstance that is better than the one we have planned.

Normally you observe people going into panic mode (experiencing anxiety, depression, anger, hate, and so forth) if anything happens against their will or their plans. This just goes to show that they are ignorant about the law of nature. Son, don't have the slightest doubt about this law. The law of gravity was just as powerful and true before Newton "discovered" it, right? Whether a given person has learned the law of gravity or not—whether he "believes in" it or not—it still works and does its job. Similarly, the law of nature is true every moment without fail, regardless of you.

It's my earnest hope you do not fall into panic mode out of ignorance.

What should you do in the situation described above? It's simple: just be calm. Relax. Take a few deep breaths and remember everything you have read in this book. Your job is to be fully aware and examine the new situations which life presents to you. If you observe enough, you can accept the reality *as it is* (which is that you have missed your flight) and not how you want it to be. If you come to terms with the reality, you soon realize that nothing in your life happens for no reason.

You might be thinking, *Okay, so what's the reason I missed my flight to my friend's wedding?*

Perhaps there's a beautiful girl who sits down next to you at the airport after missing her flight as well, and you two turn out to be soul mates. Soon you both would be thankful for missing those flights. But if you are not present in reality, you aren't aware of how many such opportunities you are missing every moment of your life.

Or perhaps, after a few hours, you learn that the plane you missed had to make an emergency landing due to a flight malfunction. As you missed that flight, you'd gotten booked onto a different flight, which caused you to reach your destination safely, and sooner than you would have, had you been on the original flight.

There are endless possibilities that can be realized *only if you accept reality the way it is and not how you want it to be.* Live life in the moment and experience every second of it. Always remember that nothing happens without the will of nature and that you are powerless against it. Fully accept the fact that anything and everything that happens is for your own good. *It's nature's way of bringing you closer to your own truth.*

Now that you understand how to live a little better, you're ready to have fun. You're ready to play the game of life, which starts in the cradle and ends in the grave. In the coming chapters, I will offer you the tools and concepts that you can use when you encounter different challenges in the game.

"Live in each season as it passes; breathe the air, drink the drink, taste the fruit, and resign yourself to the influence of the earth."

— **Henry David Thoreau, *Walden***

CHAPTER 2

FRIENDS AND ENEMIES

On any journey, it's very important that you must know who your friends and your enemies are. Similarly, on the journey of life, you must have a clear understanding of who your friends are and who your enemies.

So truth be told, **you are your own best friend as well as your worst enemy.** The sooner you come to terms with this fact, the easier it would be for you to navigate this journey of life. The difficult part is to understand how we can be both a friend and an enemy to ourselves.

You see, we are like a thermostat; if we set the thermostat to cool settings, we would blow cool pleasant air, and if we set the thermostat to the heat, we would blow hot air. Exactly in a similar manner, you have a knob to control the state in which you want to operate and based upon its settings, you can operate as your friend or you could choose to operate as your enemy. It's entirely a hundred percent your decision. You have full power & control to choose whether you want to operate as your friend in life or you want to act like your enemy.

The next most logical question which arises is, where is the knob which controls my state and how can I control it?

The knob that controls the state in which you operate lies in your thought process, the way you think and act in life. The knob lies in your moment to moment thoughts & in every action of yours. Based on your thinking and action, you generate certain kinds of feelings and emotions. Based upon the type of feelings you generate, your mind decides the operation state of yourself, either friend or enemy. *The state of mind where your dominant feelings and emotions arise through the act of truth, love & compassion, humbleness & kindness, and gratitude & forgiveness is the state of your being when you are operating as your friend.* The state of mind where your dominant feelings and emotions arise through the act of Ego, Greed, Fear, and Ignorance is the state of your being when you are operating as your Enemy.

You might ask, So why would anyone operate as their own enemy?

It's simple: out of ignorance, lack of awareness and self-introspection. Human beings have made countless attempts to understand how the external world functions, but they have failed miserably, by and large, to understand the most sophisticated machine of all—the human body-and-mind duality. They have been unable to understand their own selves. Most people do not know their own selves because they don't spend enough time getting to know their minds, their belief systems, and the workings of their inner world. Instead of being a

18

master, they are a slave to their mind and their thinking; they have no control over it.

If you put effort into understanding yourself and your inner being, your direction in life will be crystal clear to you. When you live this way, from the inside out, you will begin to see with a different set of eyes, and you will never fail to be your own best friend. Son, always remember that the highest action you can take comes from **a state of complete truth, love, compassion, humility, kindness, gratitude, and forgiveness**.

I could write a whole other book explaining the importance of your friends and the threats of your enemies, but that's for another time. For now, allow me to expound on one of your best friends (truth) and one of your worst enemies (ignorance).

Truth

Truth can have many different faces; every person may have their own definition of truth. Any number of seemingly contradictory things may be true, depending on different people's perspectives.

Let's say you are watching a sunset on the beach in Florida, and at the same time, another person is observing the sky from a beach in Japan, and another person is looking down from a shuttle in outer space. You say, "What a beautiful sunset." The guy in Japan says, "What a beautiful sunrise." And the astronaut says, "What a beautiful view of the sun and the earth."

Whose truth is the truth? Everyone is speaking truth from their perspective. The ultimate truth, in this instance, is the beauty of the natural world.

At every step in your journey, life will test you by giving you two main options to choose from. The first option will be the easy, one of false interpretation, manipulation, or half-truth, by which you can escape your problems and continue onward without hassle. By taking this option, you can overcome your imminent difficulties for a short time, but remember in the long run; you will always find yourself defeated. This option will be little you and others and turn you into your own enemy.

The second option will appear difficult, in which you have to take the side of the truth. You will know that by taking this second route, you will inevitably face the hardship of some kind, but son remember, in the end, you will always come out to be victorious. You will even feel fearful and tempted to reroute to the first option. But son, always take the side of the truth. No matter the situation at hand. Always take the side of the truth, which seems right to you morally and ethically, from the position of life where you stand. This one single message is so important that if you do not finish the rest of this book and can only take one thing away from it, it should be this: **to take the side of truth always.**

As you read this book, I have mentioned some aspects of truth from the position where I stand in life. As you navigate your own journey, it's your sole duty to find your truth as well. If you want to understand life, start by observing life as it is and not how you want it to be. Be aware of what happens to you and through you, as you will find all those events will shine a light on your own truth.

Ignorance

Let's discuss what ignorance actually is. As you grow and experience this world, you will learn new and exciting stuff. At every stage of your life, every bit of knowledge you acquire will fall into one of three buckets.

Bucket 1: things that you know that you know
Bucket 2: things that you know that you don't know
Bucket 3: things that you don't know what you don't know

Confused? Let's look at some examples.

Bucket 1: You know that you know how to talk, read, and write. You know that you are a boy, not a girl. You know that you are living on planet earth.

Bucket 2: You know that you don't know how to fly a plane or spacecraft. You know that you don't know how to hunt a lion in Africa. You know that you don't know how to run a marathon. (Or maybe you do know these things in the future! I don't know.)

Depending upon your age and the skills that you acquire, you can confidently say you know certain things and don't know other things.

Then there's the third bucket, which is what I regard as **ignorance**. After developing a few skills, reading a few books, or after starting a new enterprise, a person tends to start believing they know everything this world has to offer. They forget that this world is a vast source of knowledge and wisdom. They don't want to acknowledge that, no matter what, they will always be ignorant about the things that they don't know what they don't know.

So, as you explore this world, always keep an open mind-set. Remember that you don't know what you don't know. Never develop a sense of ego or pride after learning a few tips and tricks to "get ahead." Always be humble and close to the fact that you are a student of life. Your job is to observe it. As you have new experiences and meet new people, your first and second buckets will slowly fill up; but your third bucket will always remain empty, as you don't have the power to see into it. It's that simple.

Allow me to summarize the main lessons from this chapter for you quickly:

Controls to operate as a friend:

- ❖ Truth
- ❖ Love & Compassion
- ❖ Kindness & Humbleness
- ❖ Gratitude & Forgiveness

Controls to operate as your enemy:

- ❖ Ego
- ❖ Fear
- ❖ Greed
- ❖ Ignorance

"Strive always to excel in virtue and truth."

— **Prophet Muhammad (PBUH)**

CHAPTER 3

LIFE'S PURPOSE

Now that you are here in this world, what are you supposed to do? *What exactly is your life's purpose on this earth?*

Well actually, the cool part is, no one besides you can say what your life purpose should be. This is a question every person needs to ask themselves in one form or another. We all have to figure out how to spend our lifetime.

The next question which arises logically is, *how do I find my life purpose?*

The truth is, you never "find" or even chase your life purpose. Life will hand down your life purpose to you, to the extent of your readiness to tackle it.

Let me explain what I mean by "readiness."

When you are a kid, your life's purpose is to learn, play, and have fun. As you grow, you gain knowledge and experience. You would acquire skills that help you survive. As you acquire more and more skills, you prepare yourself to tackle life more efficiently. This is the never-ending loop, until your last day. At every stage of your life, depending upon your capabilities, life will hand down your life purpose. Your only job is to make yourself capable enough to handle it. The more capable and skillful you are, the higher is your life purpose. There is a saying in Urdu:

Khudī ko kar buland itnā ki har taqdīr se pahle Ḳhudā bande se ḳhud pūchhe batā terī razā kyā hai.

The best translation of this phrase in application to the matter at hand is, "Make yourself so capable that God, while writing your destiny, asks you "Oh! Son, what life purpose should I grant you?" (I think of "God" as "life" in this adage.)

The next logically following question is, *How do I know which skills or capabilities I should acquire?*

The answer is very simple: Just keep following your heart, your passion, your truth and your dreams and keep doing and learning the stuff which you are most passionate about.

I want to insert an important note here. The way this world works is almost never aligned with your desires. That is, you will constantly find yourself in situations where your heart says something, but something else is demanded of you. Don't fall for the trap. Do whatever it takes to follow your heart, and listen only to yourself and yourself alone and never for a single moment doubt or regret your own decisions.

Life's Purpose

But how can I know that my decisions and not others' decisions are correct for me?

Don't get me wrong, the people close to you probably have the best intentions to help you make choices. But remember that their advice is based upon their life's purpose, not yours. You can accept the support of as many people, mentors, or teachers as you wish, but always make your own decisions. Make use of your own rational & logical mind along with your heart. It matters less whether you make the right or wrong decision than whether you make it by your own free will and take total ownership and responsibility for it. And never, ever regret.

One important way of knowing you are making the right move is a feeling of fear. Before any important decision of your life, you will be fearful and hesitant to make a move. The moment you feel doubtful or hesitant, as if you are going into unknown territory, you will know you are on the right path. Growth in the direction that serves you best is not easy, and it's often scary to your nervous system, which prefers comfort and ease, but that is, undoubtedly, the correct way to move forward in life.

Fear

This world has completely misunderstood and twisted the emotion of fear. Fear is your enemy, yet it can help you—if you keep it in check and listen to it. Generally, people allow fear to rule their lives. The person who understands fear plays with it and uses it as a tool to cross the boundaries of human capabilities.

There are two categories of human beings when it comes to how to approach fear.

Category 1: At the prospect of fear, they **F**orget **E**verything **A**nd **R**un. Category 2: At the prospect of fear, they **F**ace **E**verything **A**nd **R**ise.

Make sure you fall into category 2. Never cower to your fearfulness. Life will keep throwing problems after problems at you but always smile and face them. Look for the opportunity in the problem. You will always find one. That is what will contribute to your rising.

Regret

To understand what life is all about, direct your life decisions towards your life's purpose, your passion, your truth and your dreams. Consider Bronnie Ware's book called *The Top Five Regrets of the Dying—A Life Transformed by the Dearly Departing*. Ware is an Australian nurse who spent several years caring for terminally ill patients during the last twelve weeks of their lives. She routinely asked her patients about any regrets they had or anything in their pasts they would have done differently. Ware spoke of the phenomenal clarity of vision that people gain at the end of their lives and the common themes that repeatedly surfaced during those conversations. Eventually, in her book about the experience, she identified five distinct regrets of dying people.

1. *I wish I'd had the courage to live a life true to myself, not the life others expected of me.*
2. *I wish I hadn't worked so much.*
3. *I wish I'd had the courage to express my feelings.*
4. *I wish I'd stayed in touch with my friends.*
5. *I wish that I had let myself be happier.*

Let me point out the main reasons for these regrets (my thoughts, not Ware's).

1. Fear
2. Fear and greed
3. Fear
4. Ego and greed
5. Ignorance

Son, just keep following your heart, your passion, your truth, your dreams, fearlessly, and you will look back to see a life lived with zero regrets.

"Have the courage to follow your heart and intuition. They somehow already know what you truly want to become."

— Steve Jobs

CHAPTER 4

TIME AND MONEY

N ow that you are clear about life and its purpose, let's discuss the most valuable resource you have at your disposal while you are alive. If you go around asking individuals to define this most valuable resource, you'll get a lot of different answers. A capitalist might say gold, platinum, palladium, or paper money. An environmentalist might say freshwater or clean air. The answer will vary greatly from person to person.

But the truth is that the most valuable resource available here on the earth is *time*. Everything else is in relative abundance.

As I explained earlier, people tend to live their life as if they were here for eternity. Generally speaking, they avoid grasping the simple truth that every year, month, day, hour, minute, second, which passes by, brings them nearer and nearer to their end. Perhaps we shouldn't blame them for their ignorance; however, this world is artificially designed in a way that the common man is purposely deprived of his most valuable resource.

The common man becomes miserable if someone steals his material wealth, and he might go to great lengths to recover it. But he remains ignorant about the system he lives in and of how it is stealing his most valuable lifetime away.

In the life of a common man, assuming an average length of 80 years, a modern-day education takes away a third of his lifetime. A modern-day job takes away one half of his lifetime. What is left is 20% of the lifetime at his disposal, barely, and only if he is lucky to escape the clutches of the modern day's world problems. Most people will never know where the last 20% of their lifetime disappeared to either. Life slips by in the busyness.

It's the same story in a typical day of a common adult man's life. Assuming sixteen hours of waking time per day, about half (i.e., eight hours) is spent working at a job which he dislikes. Apart from his other daily duties and habits, social media and other modern-day distractions take away the remaining half. Giant corporations are spending billions, even trillions, to get a piece of everybody's attention.

You might ask, *Why are people so ignorant?*

Again, the reason remains the same: fear of losing out in this rat race, which has no meaning. Greed and ignorance keep a common man entangled in this loop. If he were to understand the value of time and know that greed would take him nowhere, I am sure he would band together with other common men to redesign our world a little differently.

So what is the best use of my time?

It's simple. At every stage of your life, make sure your every waking second is spent following your heart, your passion, your joy and your dreams.

Money

You might say next, *But how can I follow my heart? That won't earn me a living.*

Well, that brings us to an interesting topic. Let's discuss how to think about money while you're doing your best to live purposefully.

Money is nothing but a means of exchange. Before the invention of currency, mankind exchanged goods and services for other goods and services—also known as bartering. Then, a few thousands of years ago, people started using coins as currency, and that evolved into the paper (and now digital) money we use today for the smoothest possible exchange. My point is, money keeps changing its face depending upon the era in the history of mankind. But its purpose remains consistent: to facilitate an exchange with another party in order to acquire something more valuable to you. Money in itself (paper and coins) has no value.

The ultimate value you can offer the world is your gifts and talents, something that comes from your hands or your mind. If the economy collapsed or there is a solar flare, all people that make money from the stock market will lose everything they have, with no way to gain it back, but people who have cultivated their gifts will easily be able to trade them for goods and services and rebuild society. There are tangible gifts in all of us, and the money we receive for them should only be a side-effect of their sharing and not the main goal.

Understanding this concept will make it easier for you to make money as well as spend it carefully.

So how should I make money?

At every stage of life, make use of your capabilities, skills, and talents, whatever they may be, in service to mankind in exchange for a fair amount of money. Making money is about trading a valuable gift or talent you have, preferably something you are extremely passionate about, something you would do whether you receive money for it or not. That is how you know that you are making money for the right reasons (and not from the greed of it).

And how should I use it?

Understand your vital passions and earn money to help you fulfill those passions. Exchange your money for things that contribute toward your life's purpose. These things might change with time, depending upon your interests and your life's purpose at any given stage of life. But the most expensive thing that money can ever buy is time.

The Problem with Money

People sometimes say that money is the root cause of all evil. Not true. The problem with money only arises when you give it too much importance, when you make it your primary desire. Never fall for the trap of making money for its own sake. Remember what I said in Chapter 1: you arrived empty-handed in this world, and you will leave the same way. At the end of your life, it won't matter how much money you may have accumulated. Keeping this concept in mind, you will surely have lots of fun while playing the game of money in this world.

How can I make sure I don't fall for this trap?

It's simple: always listen to your inner heart to ensure that you are making money out of love and compassion, in order to help someone else, in pursuit of a passion, to help move the human race forward, or out of curiosity to experiment with life. All these are great motives to make money.

But whenever you are driven towards money by fear and greed, you need to change track immediately. Allow me to give you some examples of how fear and greed might appear in your life.

Fear of money: a fear that you will lose your money at some point, so you keep chasing more and more of it. This might take the form of a fear of retirement, a fear of losing your job, a fear of supporting your family, and so forth.

Greed: an excessive desire to acquire more and more money so that you can afford material luxuries. Greed might involve a need to prove to others that you are rich and famous, or a need to satisfy your ego. Avoid greed of any source like a poison.

The best way to maintain a healthy view of money is to keep a check on your inner heart. Always operate from the feelings of love, compassion, kindness, and humility, and you will earn sufficient money.

"There is one kind of robber whom the law does not strike at, and who steals what is most precious to men: time."

— **Napoleon Bonaparte**

CHAPTER 5

UNDERSTANDING YOURSELF AND OTHERS

To understand yourself, you first need to understand the inner workings of this sophisticated machine, the human body. To gain mastery over it, you need to gain mastery over its most important part—the mind. And to gain mastery over your mind, you need to understand how it operates.

So, let's begin at the beginning.

When you were born, you were a blank slate, like a clean blackboard on which we (by "we" I mean our world) could write anything and whatever we wanted. All humans on this earth are born exactly the same—no inherent difference whatsoever. The only difference is the external environment in which they are born.

What are some examples of different environments? Well, let's start with geography. People are born all over the globe. Then there's socioeconomic variation—some people are born into poverty-stricken regions or communities, while others are born into wealth. There's political disparity; some people are born into democratic societies, some into socialist, and some into totalitarian regimes. People are born into every culture, caste, and religion—Jewish, Christian, Hindu, Muslim, Buddhist, and so forth—and into every historical period, such as the Middle Ages, the Industrial Revolution, the Information Age, and so forth.

As you grew and started experiencing the world around you, depending on your external situation, you slowly and steadily started filling your blackboard with the information you received. All the circumstantial information you received through your five senses (eyes (sight), ears (sound), nose (smell), mouth (taste), and skin (feel and touch)) got registered in your brain.

The way your mind saves this information is by dividing it into two buckets, likes and dislikes, based upon the positive or negative sensation you feel upon receiving the information.

The mind operates in two modes, conscious and unconscious, also referred to as the subconscious mind. All the repeated patterns and habits and "automatic" decisions that you form through time get saved into your unconscious mind; all your active decisions are processed by your conscious mind. Your mind works this way in order to save on your body's energy consumption. In a typical human, the ratio of the weight of brain to body is 1:40 (i.e., 2.5-3%), yet it consumes almost 20% of the total energy generated by your body.

This process of receiving, processing, and saving information is a continuous process, whether you are aware of it or not. As you reach adulthood, you are fully programmed with all the information you received in the past. All this information defines the self which you call "I."

"*I*" am this, "*I*" am that, "*I*" like this, "*I*" don't like that, "*I*" want this, "*I*" will do this; all this "*I*", "*I*", "*I*" is nothing but all the pre-programming done by this world and your reactions to it.

As I explained above, all the information you receive depends upon your external environment and has nothing to do with you personally. We all know, just from living in this world for a few years, that we experience billions, even trillions, of permutations and combinations of external environments and events, and so do we have a billion different types of '*I*' roaming around the earth.

This discussion brings us now to a very important question, the answer to which humans have been seeking for ages.

Who am I?

You are consciousness itself, the one who is aware of its surroundings, the one who observes and does nothing. The one who merely witnesses, is awake, and present. You are a simply conscious being and nothing else. You are not the '*I*' which has been programmed by the world.

The '*I*' which has been programmed by the world is the '*I*' who has cultivated the feeling of possessiveness of this world. The one who has attached himself with the name which was given to him by this world. The one who is fooled by the artificially designed world around him.

This way of thinking is very logical when you understand what I said in Chapter 1, that you arrived here empty-handed and will leave the same way. And since this is the case, how can you be anything which the external world has programmed you to be?

You are simply a pure consciousness and your only job is to be aware of this state. Just be aware of your surroundings, feelings, emotions, and remain equanimous. That means, do nothing.

If you understand this simple but very deep and profound concept, believe me, you will begin to see the world differently. You will begin to realize that the world and life around you are actually meaningless. It is you who gives meaning to it. I repeat, there is absolutely no meaning to life other than that which you assign to it.

Okay… you might be saying. *This all sounds overwhelming and difficult to grasp.*

I understand. If it were easy, mankind wouldn't have an unending search for this answer since the dawn of our history. To help bring you closer to this truth, I will give you two powerful and practical tips which you can implement in your daily life.

1. **Be with yourself.**

2. **Meditate.**

Be with yourself

Always spend time with yourself in solitude. Make sure, no matter your current worldly challenges, to devote time to just be with yourself and do nothing. Go outside and take a slow walk in nature. Or, if you can quiet your mind in a large crowd, just sit and observe the mass of people. Do nothing, just observe. Do not get distracted or engaged in any activity other than being with yourself. If any thoughts arise, try to resolve them logically and with the help of the lessons in this book. Using this book as your guide will surely help you.

Meditate

This is the most powerful yet largely underestimated tool. Try to feel into & learn the right techniques for meditation for you and make it a daily habit. I actually wrote this book in ten days after returning from a ten-day vipassana meditation where I was completely cut off from the external world. There I meditated from 4 a.m. to 8 p.m. in complete solitude & silence for continuous straight ten days. In my little spare time, while I was quiet and with myself, I ponder over my life. I reflected and thought about everything that I wished to share with you, my son. It was during one of those days a thought came that I have a limited time on this Earth, and I might not have enough time left to teach or share with you everything that I would love to. I realized that there is no guarantee that I won't die before I pass along all my wisdom to you. The sense of urgency drove me to write everything that I wanted to share at this stage of my life. If I were to leave this world today, I would have no regrets; I have lived my life exactly the way I have described in this book. As I write, I am enjoying this moment with the thought that one day (if nature wishes so), you will read this with a smile on your face.

Allow me to repeat a warning I gave earlier: this is what *I* did as a step towards *my* life's purpose. This is where my heart and my passion took me. Don't develop any preferences for it simply to imitate me. Follow your own heart and passion and use this book only as a guide and nothing else. You need to find your own truth.

"Knowing yourself is the beginning of all wisdom."

— Aristotle

Understanding Others

Human beings are social animals, and in order for us to navigate the journey of life, we have to interact with each other. You are not alone on your journey; after all, there are many people around you. Some are your first-degree connections, such as your parents, siblings, and close friends; others are your second-degree connections, such as your relatives, friends, and acquaintances.

Each of these people has their own personalities and behavior based upon how they have been programmed by the world. No two people are exactly alike. A set of twins who are born into the same family and are raised in the same environment may be poles apart in behavior and mindset. Because, though their external environment is the same, the way they perceive information and save it in their memories is entirely different.

Take an example of two twins seeing their mother give food to a poor person. One might perceive the joy of helping others, while the second might perceive the nuisance and hardship of being poor. What each perceives and believes becomes their reality and, in the long run, becomes their personality.

You might be saying, *Okay, I get it; everyone is unique and has their own personality and behavior. Considering our individuality, how can I best understand others?*

The truth is, you cannot and never will be able to fully and confidently understand another person.

Understanding this simple fact will save you a lot of misery that arises due to interpersonal relationships problems in everyday life. See, to understand others completely, you need to know what they are thinking precisely at a given moment, and we can never know that. Their thinking is purely based upon how they perceive and internalize the world around them. No one has control over another person's thinking, just like the two twin's example above. It is what it is.

I find it humorous to hear people say, "I understand my spouse, I understand my kids." You cannot ever understand them, or what they think, or why they think, or how they think. You have absolutely zero control and zero certainty, even if you know the person's entire history.

Ironically, people don't even understand themselves and yet seek to understand others. If you are smart enough, the odds are maybe later in your journey of life, you may begin to understand yourself. But you will never begin to understand others.

You might ask now, *Of what use is this knowledge in my journey of life?*

I'll counter with another question. Now that it is crystal clear that you will never be able to understand how others think, is there a point to act in a particular way because of what you believe others think about you?

This bears repeating: **Is there a point to do things while thinking about what others are thinking about you?**

As I said, this is a funny world we live in. Most people design their daily lives not based upon their individual dreams or preferences, but rather primarily considering what other people are thinking about them. They take any given action depending upon their expectations of others' reactions to it. They first think about what other people are thinking about them and based upon that complex logic, they decide to take action. How insane is that?

Because of this tendency, people spend their entire lives in misery, trying to understand others. They don't grasp the simple fact that no matter how hard they try, they will never be able to understand others nor please anyone all the time. There are 7.5 billion unique thinking minds roaming the planet earth. If you go on pleasing everyone, you will end up in a mental hospital.

Many don't come to this realization until they are close to their end time. Consider once more Bronnie Ware's first of five top regrets of the dying.

"I wish I'd had the courage to live a life true to myself, not the life others expected of me."

The only way a person can achieve this is if they stop wondering what others think about them. It's my earnest hope that you never waste your time in this trap. Live an authentic life true to yourself and never taint your actions with worries of what others are thinking and expecting from you. Keep following your heart, your passion, and your dreams, fearlessly, and live a life of zero regrets.

"Knowing others is intelligence; knowing yourself is true wisdom. Mastering others is strength; mastering yourself is true power."

— **Lao Tzu, *Tao Te Ching***

PART-II

APPLICATION OF
THE WISDOM

APPLICATION OF THE WISDOM

Now that you have acquired this wisdom and understand it intellectually, you need to learn how to apply it in your day-to-day life. Without proper and regular application, all the knowledge and wisdom offered in this book will serve merely as intellectual entertainment and nothing more.

The first step is to begin observing your actions and becoming totally aware of your thoughts and actions. Observe yourself carefully, question your every decision and habit, and check whether you are normally operating as a friend or an enemy to yourself.

I know that after reading thus far, you understand the need to operate in a state of truth, love, compassion, humility, and kindness; but more difficult is figuring out how to do so.

In your daily life, you spend most of your time interacting with others, right? So it's important you must know how to behave in relation to others while operating as your own friend. There will be instances that will challenge you, and there will be times that you are caught up in this life busyness. No matter how challenging the interpersonal situation, or how busy you become, always remember to follow two practical rules in your life.

Rule 1: What you think, what you say, and what you do should be exactly the same.

Rule 2: Treat and respect others exactly the way you would expect them to treat and respect you.

What I mean by "others" is every individual you encounter—from the homeless person begging on the road to the wealthy gentleman you met at some high-end social event; from the barber who cuts your hair to the CEO of a multinational company. Irrespective of race, caste, or creed of the person you meet, you need to operate exactly the same. You need to be balanced and respect everyone the same. In all, just be yourself. Do not develop a bias or favoritism toward any person or group of people based upon wealth, title, or importance they hold in society.

If you follow these two simple rules of action while interacting with others in this world, you will find it easier to operate from a state of truth, love, compassion, humility, and kindness.

The second step is to keep a very close eye on your enemies. Let me show you how you can do that.

Ego

Ego is a falsely created personality that fears death. It lives in survival mode and is fulfilled by stories of the past or desires for the future. The best way to keep a check on your ego is to remind yourself regularly of the fact that life is a short journey that will end on your deathbed. Everything that you have acquired will be left behind. Name, fame, power, success, family, friends, enemies, memories—all your worldly desires which you need to satisfy your ego—will be of no use to you in the end. So why build up your ego in the first place?

Once you can tackle this biggest enemy of all, your other enemies become very weak. You still need to keep a close watch over them, though. Let me show you how you can use your enemies for your own benefit.

Fear

Overcome fear to make progress and grow. Fear is the ego's reaction to growth and change. It is a way of self-preservation, often arising irrationally in situations where there is no immediate physical danger. Constant fear in our lives stops us from moving forward and acting in our best interest. It keeps us small. Do not allow fear to hold you back or cause you to take the path of least resistance. See and act past it. That is called courage. Have the courage to be yourself, to act on your truth, and do the right thing.

Greed

Greed is nothing but the craving of your mind and ego. Understand this nature of greed to learn the mechanics of your mind and develop an equanimous and balanced mind which neither craves nor rejects life's experiences. This will help you to enjoy your life's precious moments by being present in now and by being grateful for whatever you have. Always be centered in who you are and in your heart's true desires.

Ignorance

Never let ignorance empower you. Always be curious and excited to learn from life. Be aware that there are things you don't know what you don't know. Be humble, open, and remain teachable. Continue to be a lifelong student of life. Remember, there is always a better way to do things, and there is still something new to learn from the ever-changing life experiences and the people that surround you.

"Wisdom cannot be imparted. Wisdom that a wise man attempts to impart always sounds like foolishness to someone else ... Knowledge can be communicated, but not wisdom. One can find it, live it, do wonders through it, but one cannot communicate and teach it."

**— Hermann Hesse,
*Siddhartha***

CHAPTER 6

SUCCESS, POWER, AND HAPPINESS

There is this big misconception in our artificial world: that you will be happy if you are successful and powerful. Ask anyone for the metric of success and power, and you will hear a smorgasbord of different reasons. Some common ones are:

- Getting a promotion
- Getting a title of senior, VP, CEO
- Starting your own business
- Getting six-pack abs
- Earning a college or graduate degree
- Buying a nice house and car
- Having a fat bank account
- Being "free," or living life on one's own terms

Let me make this clear once and for all: **happiness has nothing to do with success and power.**

Ask a homeless person; he will see the person with a house and car as successful. Ask a person with a house and car; he will see the person with two houses and two cars as successful. Ask the person with two cars and two houses; he will see the person with a mansion and a luxury car as successful. Ask a millionaire; he wants to be a billionaire. Ask a billionaire; he wants to be a trillionaire.

This same principle can be applied to any success metric above. The chase is never-ending; at any stage of your life, there will always be something more out there that could increase your success or power.

That being the case, we can see that there is no end or limit to being successful. Now, if being happy is related to being successful, then no one is happy in this world, because no one considers themselves to be successful. They compare themselves to someone one step higher on the ladder. In doing so, they make their life miserable. They work hard for long hours, always in a state of stress. They have made this a norm in their life: work hard to be successful. Even if they do achieve success (not in their eyes, but in the eyes of others), they continue to slog and work hard to achieve even more success. There's no simple understanding of where this madness ends—the truth is in the grave. The main reason for this madness is greed. People have made greed their primary modus operandi, not knowing that all the time they were chasing success, they were operating as an enemy and not as a friend to themselves.

So the most logical question you will ask is, *How can I be successful and powerful, and at the same time be happy?*

You are a smart kid, aren't you?

Success

Success should be the byproduct of your hard work, not the other way around. Understand this concept very clearly: success should not be the goal. Don't work hard to be successful, but work hard because you want to. Work hard at your dreams and passion. Don't work hard to prove anything to anyone else or to achieve something like power, name, or fame. The only person you need to prove anything to, is yourself and no one else.

The definition of success should be tailored to you; there's no one-size-fits-all version. It can be anything that you define as success for yourself and not what this world has defined for you.

Say you want to learn how to code and become a great software engineer. Don't spend your time and money getting a college degree simply to be able to prove to others that you are now a software engineer. That is a success as defined by this artificial world. You can be the best software engineer out there without any college degree at all. If you work hard and you know it in your heart that you are the best and you have a true passion for your craft, you should feel successful, you don't need any validation for it. Now, if you genuinely believe that going to college and learning this craft will be of great benefit for you and your life purpose, go ahead and enroll. But your success is not dependent on any certificates, it only relies on your ability and willingness to learn and dedicate energy towards what you are passionate about.

Power

People associate power with the worldly title they hold. They flaunt their clout by asserting, "I am a senior partner," or "I am a director over hundreds of employees," or "I am a millionaire." But this is not power; it is a mere title with no real substance.

True power does not lie in displaying or boasting of your power, but rather in knowing your level of capability in relation to the work that needs to be done or that you want to do. It is about knowing that you are capable, that you understand yourself, and that you use your passion in tandem with the will of nature to forward your life purpose. That's true power. True power lies in your heart and in your self-confidence, not in what the outside world assumes about you.

Let me explain further what I mean by "true power."

You might be a millionaire who drives an expensive car and lives in a mansion. But deep inside, you know the truth: that you are in debt thousands of millions of dollars which you owe to banks, lenders, and others.

Or, you might be a "common person" (by the definition of this world) who lives in a small apartment and knows deep in your heart that you can buy anything—whenever and whatever you wish—but you choose not to. You have the choice of having things, and you use it wisely and with love rather than with greed. In this case, you have true power.

Let me reiterate: true power lies in your heart and in your self-confidence, not in titles and appearances and others' beliefs about you.

How can I develop such self-confidence?

Well, self-confidence is the natural state of human beings. You were born with it. Yes! That's right, you already have self-confidence built-in you since the time you were born. While you were a child exploring your environment, you were fearless and full of self-confidence— until this world started pushing its rules to interfere and reprogram you. Because of external influences and the artificial world we live in, you somehow lost your self-confidence. So truth to be told, you do not need to develop your self-confidence; you need to figure out the reason why you lost it.

The main reasons people lose their self-confidence are **competition** and **comparison**. The world is designed in such a way that it promotes these two problems within almost all its established systems. From kindergarten through university, children are graded and taught to be competitive through constant comparison of their achievements with their peers'. The same is true when they enter the workforce. Due to the competitive nature of this world, people compare themselves to others and consequentially desire to be like others. When they are not able to reach the level they perceive their peers to have achieved, they slowly start to lose self-confidence. They don't realize the simple fact that their only competition and their only competitors are they themselves and no one else.

Life is the only game in which, after reaching the finish line, people realize that they were the sole player in the game and had no competition whatsoever other than themselves. I earnestly wish that you won't find yourself making this realization later in your life. Don't wait until you reach the finish line to realize this simple truth.

So, what is the ideal way to achieve success, power, and happiness in this world?

Remember the lessons learned earlier in this book about the law of nature and life's purpose. Nothing happens against the will of nature. Your only job is to make yourself capable enough that life can grant you the right powers. As long as you keep operating as your own friend in this world, nature will make sure you are given the proper powers at the right time. It will be your duty to use them well. You can use them in the service of others, or you can use them to satisfy your own self-need.

If you use them in the service of others, you will act with your "friend faculties" of love, compassion, kindness, and humility. If you use your powers and capabilities for your selfish needs, you will help your enemies—ego, greed, fear, and ignorance. Depending upon how you keep using your current power, your future power is decided by nature.

Make sure you keep a close watch on how you operate in your daily life. Life is simple, but people make it complicated. Work hard on things that you love doing, things you are most passionate about. If you keep following this simple rule, happiness will be the byproduct of your day-to-day actions, and success will be the byproduct of your day-to-day work. Now go play and have fun out there!

"For what shall it profit a man, if he gain the whole world, and suffer the loss of his soul?"

— **Jesus Christ**

CHAPTER 7

CREATING YOUR OWN LIFE

In order for you to be the creator of your own life, you need to thoroughly grasp two powerful effects that occur in your life. Developing your knowledge of these two effects will make it easier for you to follow your dreams and passions and achieve whatever your heart desires. They are called the "compound effect" and the "butterfly effect."

The Compound Effect

The compound effect is a concept that can only be understood if you observe it very carefully in your daily life. It's difficult to grasp it intellectually, so try to do so empirically. For the compound effect to reveal its power, the only factor required is time.

Let's look at some instances of the compound effect in action.

Say there is bucket sitting beneath a tap. From that tap water is dripping, a single drop at a time. If you keep observing this slow process, something very magical happens over time. The bucket fills up.

You might say, *What's magical about that?*

Well, as I said, it's difficult to truly understand this idea intellectually; you need to observe it yourself. The bucket's transition from empty to full is due to the compound effect.

Let's take another example. Say you plant a seed in the soil. You water it and ensure it gets sunlight every day. If you keep doing so consistently, the seed will sprout, and over the years, it grows into a tree (depending on what type of seed it is, of course!). The transition from seed to a tree is due to the compound effect.

Let's look at the construction of a skyscraper, starting from a barren lot and ending as a tower that boasts a hundred floors. By placing a foundation of one brick at a time, the building rises from nothing until it reaches high into the sky. The transition from barren land to the skyscraper is due to the compound effect.

How can the compound effect benefit me?

You saw in the above examples how something was manifested from nothing. Similarly, to achieve your dreams and passions, you have to keep working at them consistently. Keep adding drop by drop or brick by brick. By the power of compound effect and the will of nature, your goal will surely manifest. But remember, for the compound effect to accomplish its magic, it needs time. As you know very well, time is the most valuable resource you have on this earth. So make sure while you navigate the journey of your life that whatever desires you decide to pursue are worth your time.

Let me share with you a very powerful hack to expedite the power of the compound effect. It's called the "exponential compound effect."

Exponential Compound Effect

To introduce the power of the exponential compound effect, let's play a small game.

I give you thirty seconds to choose one of the following two options:

Option 1: You accept an offer of $100,000 in cash today.

Option 2: You accept an offer of a penny today and starting tomorrow, I will double your holdings every day for the next thirty days.

Take only thirty seconds to choose either option.

Now that you have made a choice, let's look at both options carefully.

With Option 1, you get $100,000 in cash in an instant. That's simple and straightforward. You have cash in hand and zero time wasted. That's not a bad choice.

Now, for the curious mind who turned down the temptation of instant gratification and went for Option 2: let's figure out how much of a fool they made themselves. Check out the table below.

Day	Exponential compounding in action	Day	Exponential compounding in action
0	$0.01	16	$655.36
1	$0.02	17	$1,310.72
2	$0.04	18	$2,621.44
3	$0.08	19	$5,242.88
4	$0.16	20	$10,485.76
5	$0.32	21	$20,971.52
6	$0.64	22	$41,943.04
7	$1.28	23	$83,886.08
8	$2.56	24	$167,772.16
9	$5.12	25	$335,544.32
10	$10.24	26	$671,088.64
11	$20.48	27	$1,342,177.28
12	$40.96	28	$2,684,354.56
13	$81.92	29	$5,368,709.12
14	$163.84	Bingo!	$10,737,418.24
15	$327.68		

Starting from *a* single penny, you make more than **$10 million in thirty days!** That right there is the power of the exponential compound effect.

So what just happened? How did penny turn into more than $10 million? Well, let's take a close look at the exponential compound effect and how can we unleash its power in our lives.

First, check out the graph below, which plots the transition of a penny to $10 million.

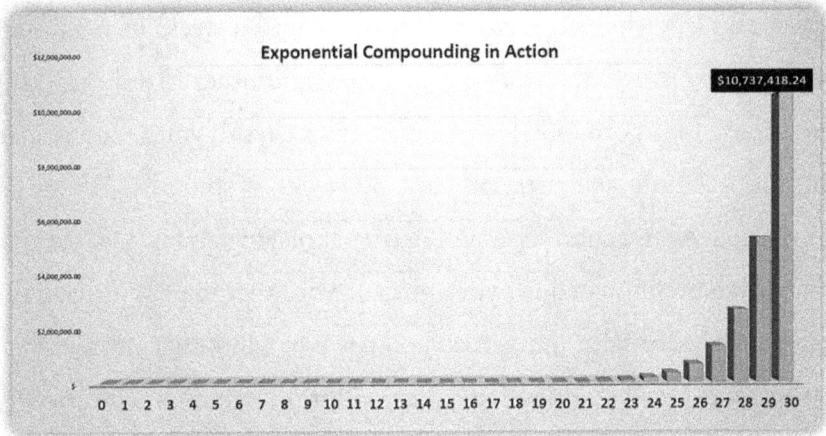

Exponential Compounding in Action

$10,737,418.24

0 1 2 3 4 5 6 7 8 9 10 11 12 13 14 15 16 17 18 19 20 21 22 23 24 25 26 27 28 29 30

Do you observe the pattern? Between Days 1 and 23, you hardly see any movement at all; but starting on Day 24, you can observe remarkably fast growth. This is where the true power of exponential compounding effect lies.

Now, how can you unleash the power of this effect in your life?

Well, just as with the compound effect, you can use the exponential compound effect to increase your capability in any field or skill set in order to follow your dreams. The secret ingredient required to unleash the power of exponential compound effect, however, is in *incremental efforts* over a certain period of time. This is the very powerful hack you can use alongside the plain old compound effect.

Let's learn more about this hack.

Say you want to learn how to play the guitar. All you need to do is learn one new chord every day. (Or one chord a week, to make sure you perfect it.). Once you perfect it, learn another chord and keep practicing the chords you learned on former days. If you are consistent in this practice for the next 30 days, 30 weeks, 30 months, or even 30 years, you will for sure, become a master at playing guitar. Decide your own time period based on your goal. If you wish merely to have fun and experiment with the guitar, perhaps you will only continue for a short time; but if you develop a passion for it, you might continue for the rest of your life. The more you keep practicing your skills, the more you will improve. There is no limit to how great you can become.

You can use the power of this effect towards any goal you set your heart on. If you want to learn any sport, start any business, create any piece of art, invent any machine of any kind, get in shape, develop personally, change your habits, improve your personal relationships—

just make sure you keep taking incremental, consistent steps in the direction of whatever you desire. You do not have to make giant leaps; take baby steps but do so consistently. Always remember, *"A journey of a thousand miles begins with a single step."* - (Lao Tzu, a Chinese philosopher).

To be the best version of yourself, do not set any limits on yourself. Always remember that humans are bounded only by the laws of nature. So keep following your heart. Also, never compare or compete with others. Your only competition is with yourself: so become a better version of yourself each day compared to the day before. If you keep adding and improving on yourself by a mere 1% each day, over time and by the power of exponential compound effect, you will become capable enough to fulfill all your dreams and desires.

Never forget where the true power of the exponential compound effect lies. Look back at the graph—we didn't see any noticeable gains until Day 24. Similarly, as you encounter difficulties on your journey, you have to be patient and trust the law of nature and the power of the exponential compound effect. Do not make a habit of giving up too early before allowing the effect a chance to show its power. Your only job is to persevere at doing what you love and leave the rest upon the will of nature. Life will decide the best time for the exponential compound effect to unleash its power.

Butterfly Effect

In creating your own life, the other effect you need to be aware of is the butterfly effect. The term originated in a sci-fi short story called *A Sound of Thunder* by American writer Ray Bradbury. It is a story of how the killing of a single butterfly thousand years in the past completely altered present and future events in the world.

The way I view the butterfly effect is very comparable to two established laws of physics working in conjunction:

1. Newton's third law, which states that for every action, there is an equal and opposite reaction.

And,

2. The first law of thermodynamics, also known as the law of conservation of energy, which states that energy can neither be created nor destroyed. It can only be transferred or changed from one form to another.

Let's see how these laws are applicable in your life.

When you take any action—be it physical, verbal, or mental—it has some sort of equal (and perhaps opposite) reaction, depending upon the nature of your action. Once an action is conducted, its effects are out there in nature. The energy or vibrations created by your action, whether positive or negative, will continually reverberate in nature, and it will be a deciding factor in your future experiences in life.

For any positive actions which are conducted in a state of truth, love, compassion, humility, kindness, gratitude, and forgiveness, there will be positive outcomes, either instantly or sometime in the future.

Let's look at an instance of the butterfly effect in action in your life. Imagine one day you are in a hurry to meet up with someone important. As you walk down the road, you see a poor kid selling newspapers. You feel something in your heart for him, and out of a state of love and compassion, you help him by purchasing all his newspapers. The kid thanks you and happily goes home early that day. On his way home, he stops to purchase some flowers for his mother. While he is purchasing the flowers, he sees a car speeding up the road and a woman crossing the road, unaware of the car's approach. The kid immediately jumps into the road and pulls the woman out of harm's way. To relax and calm the women down, he gives her two roses and continues homeward. The woman, thanks the kid for saving her life and, in a state of gratitude, continues on her way towards a nearby park where she is about to meet with the love of her life. When she enters the park, she smiles and gives you her two roses.

Son, this is the power of the butterfly effect.

Through your knowledge and awareness of these two powerful effects, you can be the active creator of your own life. You can use them to your advantage to design your dream life. Being aware of the importance of daily incremental efforts will significantly help you in your journey of life. Always keep in mind that any small action today can change the course of your history. This mindset will help you to make wise and right decisions. At any stage in your life, whenever you are in doubt, just follow a simple rule: *make sure to operate as a friend to yourself, in a state of truth, love, compassion, kindness, humility, gratitude, and forgiveness.* Doing this, you can rest assured that both the effects of nature are working toward your own good.

"It's the action, not the fruit of the action, that's important. You have to do the right thing. It may not be in your power, may not be in your time, that there'll be any fruit. But that doesn't mean you stop doing the right thing. You may never know what results come from your action. But if you do nothing, there will be no result."

— **Mahatma Gandhi**

CHAPTER 8

ARTIFICIAL WORLD

I have made quite liberal references to the artificiality of our world thus far in this book, so it's important that I elaborate a bit on this term. In fact, I won't just share my views but will tell you the secret of seeing through this artificiality to the truth.

The secret to uncovering the truth is this: every time you encounter any process, belief, system, or ideology in this world while you navigate the journey of your life, always ask one simple question:

Why?

Just by asking *why* and using your calm, rational, and logical mind to provide an answer, you will start to unlock the flaws in many worldly systems. And once you start seeing things differently than the rest of the herd, you will understand how and why humans have created an artificial world around them.

Let's look at some of the major systems humans have created. Allow me to share how I view them, though I hope that you will come to your own conclusions and judgments about them.

The Modern-Day Education System

In the last hundred years or so, we have created a pattern which we can even call a norm at this point: Every kid has to go to school, then high school, then college. Parents believe this is the default way of life for their children and they never question why it is perpetuated.

In fact, people give you a blank face if you ask them why kids must undergo so many years of schooling. If they do provide an answer, they probably say that "Everyone does it" or "It's just the way it is."

Pushing them further, you might ask why again. But why?

They will answer so that they can get good grades, get into the right college, and get a good job. So that they make a living as their parents do, and then they can repeat the same process for their children.

I find this thinking very difficult to digest. Does a person really need a certificate from some external source like a college to tell them that they are all of a sudden capable of doing something? As if immediately following the graduation ceremony, they are able to read and write at some arbitrarily specific level and perform at some arbitrarily specific job? Why not before the graduation ceremony?

People can learn anything they set their hearts and mind to. For example, if I want to write a book, I do not need 4 years diploma in English literature to do so. If I want to learn about engineering, I can volunteer my time at an engineering firm, or I can study online. With the invention of the internet, it has become laughably easy to acquire knowledge in any subject. You are in full control of how you want to design your life, including your education. You need no approval from any external source to verify your capabilities. You have all the tools, as well as the self-awareness that you need to make yourself capable enough. Great minds in the world like Elon Musk didn't get a master's in aero science or mechanical engineering before founding his company SpaceX—he read books and taught himself. It's so simple.

You might be wondering how I came to this realization. Well, I am too a product of our modern education system and its biggest joke. I have a B.E. in electronics and a master's in engineering management. I possess a certificate so that if anyone questions me, I can prove my credentials. It even easily got me a job in my field. Another big joke is, according to the modern class ranking system, I was named a distinctive student of electronics and engineering management with a 3.5 GPA, not because I was good at the subject but only because I was good at memorizing without understanding. What a joke! I hardly remember any theory I was taught, as I wasn't interested in that stuff. Yes, I was fascinated with the electronics and internet revolution happening around me, but I was more interested in practical application than in the actual science. As long as I was able to connect two wires and see a light bulb glow, I was happy.

Okay, I understand your point, but I really want to go after this one-year master's program at this prestigious university. I think this is my passion, my calling. Should I do it?

Do it—*if* you answer this question in the affirmative: If I were to tell you that you had only one year left to live, would you still go and get this degree?

If yes, by all means, go and get it. But if you have the slightest doubt, rethink and reevaluate the true intentions behind your calling.

My advice for you is, don't fall into the trap of this broken education system. The world is your university and life is your teacher. Explore other, creative ways to gain experience and knowledge. Seek knowledge for the right reason—seek it out of love and passion for it, and not because society had made it a norm. Just follow your heart, your passion and your dreams, fearlessly, to learn and experience the vastness out there.

The Modern-Day Global Economic System

Looking at the entire global economic system, I seriously doubt the true intentions of the collective human race. It looks like we have picked up the hammer and thrown it on our own feet.

Let me explain what I mean by asking some *why* questions.

Why is the salary of a manager, a VP, or a CEO of a soda pop manufacturing company higher than that of a trash collector or a nurse practitioner who cares for the sick in a hospital? I mean, what greater social impact do high-salary corporate executives have on society and the lives of the millions of people around them?

Let's compare two scenarios and their impact on society.

Scenario 1: All the VP's at a soda pop manufacturing company go on strike.

Scenario 2: All the garbage collectors and nurses at a hospital go on strike.

Which scenario would have a more negative impact on society and other individuals' lives?

The answer is most likely in Scenario 2. In fact, Scenario 1 might actually benefit society as there would be less of the unhealthy soda pop products consumed.

Let's ask some more *why* questions to find some more anomalies in our economy.

Why does following a noble profession such as medicine come with a huge price tag? The most important action a person can conduct here on Earth is to save someone else's life. Despite knowing the value of human life, this world has put a heavy financial burden on anyone who wants to pursue the profession of a doctor. Today doctors are in constant worry about paying off their substantial student loans. Imagine the state of mind of a doctor who is carrying out his duties not out of passion and love for his patients but under the weight of the loan which he has to repay to this world. In fact, this is true for most of the modern day professions requiring a higher degree that anyone wants to pursue.

The way our world has designed the modern incentive system is encouraging people to work towards personal gain and not towards helping society and moving the human race forward. Because of this culture, people wake up each day with the thought in mind of how I can compete with my peers and get ahead in this rat race? How can I crush my competition so that I can maximize my personal gain?

Alternatively thinking, how about we design a world where people are incentivized based upon the social impact they bring to society? Imagine people getting paid for helping others or improving others' living conditions. Imagine people waking up every day with the only thought, how I can help my fellow human beings so that I improve my own life and self as well? Surely we could have built a paradise here on the earth; instead, just look around what we have done to this world.

The Modern-Day Concept of Living

This is another modern-day madness that we humans have made our lives' default. Get a job, make a living, buy a house, and save for retirement. Nothing but another crazy yet normalized invention of this world.

Let's ask why again. Why should I get a job? Why buy a house? Why save for retirement? Why retire at age sixty-five?

Let's look at this concept from an alternate angle and answer the inverted question: why not structure your life differently?

Job

Why not earn a living by working for yourself? Why doesn't the education system teach us how to be self-sufficient and earn a living by doing something all by yourself? Why is there so little focus in classes on how to make money, invest money, and grow one's money using your own talents? You are paying educators to teach you how to get a degree so that you can work for someone else and make money for them.

House

The way I see the modern-day concept of buying a house is that it's a prison. Let me ask, how would you feel if I were to take away your freedom and imprison you for 30 years? Not only would I put you in prison, but I'd also charge you for living in it. But wait, we humans take this one level higher. We build a prison around ourselves. We pay someone else in order to put ourselves behind bars, and then we keep paying them for thirty years so that they don't kick us out of our own prison. For most people, this is the case. They buy small condos or apartments with expensive mortgages and keep paying someone else for 30 years so that they don't lose their living space.

Mankind seems to have forgotten that nature has provided us the whole planet to live on and roam freely. Sure, having a house for yourself and your family as your own sanctuary is a wonderful thing. But modern society has taken this concept of owning a house to the extreme.

We don't see that we have 15.77 billion acres of habitable land available for 7.7 billion people, which gives us each approximately 2 acres, which is 87,120 square feet to live on. Yet we are satisfied by a mere fraction of it; the typical house size is 3000 square feet or even less, which is next to nothing compared to the total habitable land on earth. The cramped spaces have restricted our freedom, not only our physical freedom but our minds and hearts as well. We have created borders around our lands, cities, states and countries, but the main underlying problem is that we have created borders around our minds. We have blocked our minds from thinking differently.

Retirement

Why should I retire only once I am sixty-five? Why not now? Why not live an entire life as if I am retired and free?

What is the definition of retirement, according to today's standards? Well, after you slog for more than two-thirds of your life, you finally get to enjoy the fruits of your hard work through the savings you (hopefully?) have built. The people who act and think this way exist in an illusion. They live in some alternate reality where life will be magically perfect once they punch out for the final time. They don't live in the present but instead in a distant future reality where they believe their real life, love, and freedom will happen and they can finally live peacefully. If owning a house is a prison, the concept of retirement is like slavery. Refer back to Chapter 1 to refresh the simple concept that we must live moment to moment to enjoy our lives.

"To enjoy life, enjoy this moment, to live life, live this moment."

There is nothing more precious, more real, more abundant and more readily available to you than this moment. If you want to travel, do it now. If you want to move to a tropical place, do it now. If you want to feel at peace, feel it now. Don't wait for later when you are older. Your time on this Earth is not guaranteed. Again, if I told, you have one year to live, would you still save for retirement or would you enjoy the fruits of your life now? If you enjoy them now, more will come. More will always come. You will always be supported by life as long as you are rooted in your purpose, talents, and all the goodness in your heart. Nature wants to work with you, not against you. Only the world tells you that nature is against you and that you have to fight for your survival and hoard or save money for later years. It is an illusion. Have faith in nature for being provided and work on the things that make you happy. This way, you will feel "retired" your whole life. And more than that, you will be free.

The Modern-Day Religions

Ask anyone this question: Why do you adhere to the tenets of Christianity, Judaism, Buddhism, Hinduism, Islam, or whichever religious system you hold to?

The most common answer you'll get: Because I was born into a family that practiced it.

Poor humans, they never had any choice, and now they're trapped for the rest of their lives. Let's take this topic lightly, as it seems that most get emotional when addressing their religion.

So, why follow any specific religion? When you examine them, you realize that, despite their differences, one thing they generally have in common is the idea of an afterlife and going to heaven. Over our entire history, mankind has never come to a logical conclusion about whose god is the actual god. So far, I haven't met a single person who died and came back to confirm which set of beliefs allows you entrance into heaven.

I sometimes jokingly ask myself: when there is a buffet of religions out there, why settle for only one? Follow everything or whichever components of all that makes the most logical sense. At least after I die, I can be 100% sure of gaining entry pass from one of the gods who actually rules the kingdom of heaven.

Here one practical tip: ask any person living on this earth if he wants to go to heaven. He will jump for joy and say, "Hell yeah!" Then ask him if he wants to die in order to get there. You will receive a different answer.

Well, don't take anything very seriously in this world. Just observe, experience, smile, have fun, and keep following your heart, your passions, and your dreams, fearlessly. If you want to follow any religion or practice out of love for it, do it. Keep a check on your feelings, though. Don't subscribe to any mindset out of fear of social pressure and any religious authority. Follow whatever you would like, but by your own free will and because you wish to and not because you have to.

"Wisdom is not a product of schooling but of the lifelong attempt to acquire it."

— **Albert Einstein**

CHAPTER 9

HOW TO BRING THE CHANGE

After living on this earth for some time and encountering at least a few unpleasant experiences, you might have thought of doing something about the difficulties you regularly face.

You might have questions such as,

What if I want to change the outdated systems and beliefs of this world?

What if I want to help someone understand?

What if I want to inspire change in my parents, friends, spouse, colleagues, and so forth?

These are excellent thoughts and motivation for helping others. You can have all the good intentions to help others, but the truth is, the only thing you can change is yourself. Not to sound cliché, but you need to be the change that you would like to see in this world.

What do I mean by this? Well, let's get into the root of the problem first.

Let's say you are happy doing what you are doing. For example, you are really happy with your school or your job. You are really happy with the relationships you have with your friends, parents, colleagues, teachers, and girlfriend or wife. Surrounded by this happiness, is it likely that you will harbor these desires to change the world around you?

My guess is the answer is probably no. The only time that such thoughts of change arise is when we are unhappy with our circumstances. When our external environment is not the way we would like it to be, we start developing an aversion towards it. We start making efforts to change it. We even get angry, frustrated, and miserable. And we believe that we can be happy once we fix our external environment. Right?

Do you see the problem here?

We humans live our entire lives, trying to fix our external environment. For example, a husband says, "If only my wife would do this, this, and this, I would be very happy." A wife says, "If only my husband would do this, this, and this, I would be very happy." A child says, "If only my parents would understand me," and parents say, "If only our son or daughter would understand us." This same concept is seen in almost all aspects of human life, and this is the root cause of our unhappiness.

We keep trying to fix our external environment to bring the change, unaware that we have zero control over anything outside the boundary of our bodies. You may want to believe you can control and change your external environment, but the truth is, you cannot. And when all your attempts fail, you become frustrated and angry, you develop hatred, and without realizing it, you start operating as your own enemy.

Always remember this golden rule: *The only person you can change is yourself. The problem that you need to fix lies within yourself. If you genuinely and truly want to bring a change, you first need to be that change.*

The next logical question is, *How can I be that change?*

It's simple: just understand yourself first. (You may wish to reread that chapter.)

Now you might say, What if I want to change the world in the service of mankind? What if I am already happy and content in life, but I truly want to help others?

The only way you can achieve this is by **selflessly acting** for the good of others instead of yourself. You cannot mix your own selfish desire or greed with a wish to change the world for others' sake. If you can pick any cause in this world that you are passionate about making a difference in, make sure you do so by acting selflessly for the cause and not to achieve any worldly pleasure, or fame, wealth. Living a life of such passion is undoubtedly a very noble way to live in this world.

One way to make yourself capable of such greatness is to learn all you can about all the latter great people across history, from Jesus to the prophet Mohammed to Gautama Buddha, Mother Teresa to Gandhi, Nelson Mandela to Dr. Martin Luther King, Jr. Learn from their lives and look for the patterns and causes they stood for in order to bring about positive change in society.

You can use this advice for any goal you set your heart on. Always develop a habit of learning from true masters. The true masters are the people who are accomplishing or have already accomplished something that you wish to do as well. They will be the guiding light for your journey towards a similar goal and give you a foundation so that you don't have to reinvent the wheel. For example, if you would like to know more about science, mathematics, spirituality, business, or economics, you need to learn from the people who have already walked that path. Always look out for experienced mentors who can help you in your life journey. If you cannot meet them in person, the second-best options are books. Develop the habit of acquiring knowledge by reading the works of true masters.

Now, this advice is for learning purposes only. Do not try to imitate someone you are not. Make sure you live an authentic life true to yourself. Follow your heart and your own passions. You can always learn from others whom you admire and who have more experience than you in whatever area you desire to know more, but at the end of the day, always do your own thinking and follow what your heart desires. Also, always keep a check on your feelings, and no matter what, you keep operating from a state of truth, love, compassion, humility, kindness, gratitude, and forgiveness.

"Yesterday I was clever, so I wanted to change the world. Today I am wise, so I am changing myself."

— **Rumi**

CHAPTER 10

HOW TO WIN THE GAME OF LIFE

At this point, you're thinking, *Cool! I get it. I get that life is the journey straight to death, and the way I need to live is to play the game of life with myself. I understand the value of time and my life's purpose. I understand that this is an artificial world around me, and I am slowly beginning to understand myself and how my mind operates. But how do I make sure that I come out a winner in this game?*

Great question, and it doesn't even require a lengthy response.

The day you were born is the day you started to play this game. You came out crying in this world while everyone around you was smiling with joy.

If you want to be a winner, remember this: on the day you leave this world, if you are the only one who is smiling with joy and everyone around you is crying, that's a great indication that you have won the game of life.

Son, as I write my final words of this book, in my heart, I am feeling deep love and pain both at the same time. Love, for the time that I have spent with you through the pages of this book, for which I am immensely grateful to nature for giving me this opportunity. Pain, as the time has come that I need to depart and move ahead on the journey of my own life. I so wish I could stay with you forever to guide you along the journey of your life, but you need to navigate your journey on your own.

Two things that I would like to leave behind with you is this book and the five commandments you need to win the game of life. I also call it a blueprint to win the game of life. Keep reminding yourself of these five commandments every second of your active life. If its nature's will, I am two hundred percent confident that you will come out as a champion of this game.

THE FIVE COMMANDMENTS

The blueprint to win the game of life

1. *Live your life as a journey straight towards death.*

2. *Remember that the nature of life is impermanence.*

3. *Know that the law of nature ensures that nothing happens against nature's will.*

4. *Act selflessly and without regard to ego.*

5. *Think in a state of truth, love, compassion, humility, kindness, gratitude and forgiveness.*

"Life is too short to waste, so enjoy it...!!!"

– Dad

Conclusion

Now that I have read this book and know all about life, am I all set for the journey? I don't have to worry about anything else, right?

That's your ignorance talking. What you have got from this book is the knowledge about the wisdom, not the wisdom itself.

Think about this book the following way: a man did all the work of finding suitable farmland, planting a crop of sugarcane, and harvesting it. After harvest, he crushed the sugarcane to extract the juice and threw away the waste. He filtered and purified the juice to produce the sweetest and purest drop out of the whole crop for himself to taste.

What you got from this book is a description of the taste of that purest and sweetest drop of sugarcane juice—not an actual taste. But now it's your turn to use the concepts given in this book to find your own land and grow your own sugarcane so that you can taste the juice for yourself. In other words, remember that this book is only a guide. You have to walk the path yourself; no one else can do it for you. You have to find your own truth.

Why do I have to seek the truth, and what is the higher or ultimate truth?

On the topic of the higher truth or ultimate truth, I don't know what I don't know. I can only speak from a position of life where I stand. The only way humans can become enlightened is when they overcome their ignorance. The only way they can overcome their ignorance is by knowing the ultimate truth. The beauty is everyone is standing at a different position in their life and ignorant in their own unique way. The only way we have a chance to become enlightened is to strive for the truth else; we will accept our ignorance as our reality. So it's my logical understanding, if every human strives for the ultimate truth, they would have a higher chance to overcome their ignorance and dwell as a higher enlightened being.

How can I start loving life and not fear death?

Let me give you a practical tip: make it a point to attend funerals as often as possible. After observing death so closely, you will lose your fear of death. Doing this will also remind you continually about the fragility and impermanence nature of life and keep you tied to reality. By following this routine, you will start to see life face to face. You will slowly come to the realization that the time you have is a true blessing, and you will be inspired to use it wisely. At that point, you are bound to fall in love with life.

ACKNOWLEDGEMENTS

I truly want to thank the supreme nature, who has blessed me with this beautiful life and by a miraculous turn of events, has allowed me to encounter its wisdom.

To my reader: what an incredible journey it has been thus far. I apologize if I have unintentionally (or intentionally) hurt your feelings at any point in this book, and I sincerely ask for your forgiveness. With all the humility and love in my heart, I thank you for being such a wonderful friend of mine on this journey. I understand you have given me your most precious possession, i.e., your time, and honestly, I do not have anything relatively valuable enough to give back to you. All I have is my prayers and well wishes that all your dreams and desires in this world are fulfilled. May you find your truth and spread your wisdom, love, and happiness to everyone around you. It is my earnest hope that this book can serve you as a guide in fulfilling your dreams, as it has for me.

I would like to take this opportunity to thank all the prophets who have walked on this planet earth. I thank all the spiritual masters from His Holiness the Dalai Lama to Sadhguru to His Holiness Late Syedna

Mohammed Burhanuddin for their spiritual support. I thank every legend who left their impression on this world, from Mahatma Gandhi to Steve Jobs, who showed us what human beings can accomplish. I thank all the great authors who have shared their wisdom through their written works.

I thank every single person whom I have met in my life and have taught me something about life. I thank each and every family member, friends, and colleagues whose interactions have helped me understand what life is all about.

Lastly, I would like to thank my wife, Humera, who shows me every day what love really looks like. Without her unbiased, nonjudgmental, relentless love, this book wouldn't have been possible.

Thank you, life!
Mohammed Hakim

ABOUT THE AUTHOR

MOHAMMED HAKIM

is an eternal student of life and advocate of positive change with a vision to awaken people to their infinite potential so they can build the life of their dreams. Mohammed honestly believes that his life is worth living if he can change other people's lives with his ideas, writings, and books. He's gifted with a vision that can inspire individuals to portray the image of who you are and what you want to achieve from the inside out. He is the author of the book "Wisdom Worth Spreading." A book loaded with wisdom, which is the result of his relentless quest to find answers to life's most difficult questions. He is on a mission to empower, inspire, and awaken as many people as possible. An entrepreneurial spirit who is deeply dedicated to sharing his wisdom, he is also of the belief that we only have a limited amount of time on this beautiful planet, and we should live that life we're given to the fullest. Through sharing the wisdom he has acquired along his journey, he also feels driven to make this world a better place than when he first entered. When he isn't inspiring others, Mohammed enjoys being in the great outdoors, exploring, learning new things, and reading inspiring books. Above all, he loves spending time with his precious newborn kids and lovely wife.

If you have any questions or feedback about the book, please reach out to Mohammed at the below email address.

Contact Info:

Website: www.wisdomworthspreading.com
Email: mohammed@wisdomworthspreading.com
Twitter Handle: WisdomWorthSpreading (@WWS_wisdom)

www.ingramcontent.com/pod-product-compliance
Lightning Source LLC
Chambersburg PA
CBHW020508030426
42337CB00011B/279